Pebble

Co

China

by Christine Juarez

Consulting Editor: Gail Saunders-Smith, PhD

CAPSTONE PRESS

a capstone imprint

Pebble Books are published by Capstone Press,
1710 Roe Crest Drive, North Mankato, Minnesota 56003
www.capstonepub.com

Library of Congress Cataloging-in-Publication Data
Juarez, Christine, 1976–
  China / by Christine Juarez.
    pages cm.—(Pebble Books. Countries)
  Includes bibliographical references and index.
  Summary: "Simple text and full-color photographs illustrate the land, animals, and people of
China"—Provided by publisher.
  ISBN 978-1-4765-3517-3 (paperback)
  1. China—Juvenile literature. I. Title.
  DS706.J83 2014
  951—dc23
2013002012

Editorial Credits
Erika L. Shores, editor; Bobbie Nuytten, designer; Wanda Winch, media researcher;
Jennifer Walker, production specialist

Photo Credits
Capstone, 4; Dreamstime: Hanhanpeggy, 15, Yunhao Zhang, 11; Shutterstock: AKaiser, cover,
1 (scalloped design), beboy, 17, fotohunter, cover, Hung Chung Chih, 9, JinYoung Lee, 19,
Ohmega1982, back cover globe, Oleg_Mit, 22 (bill), ra3rn, 22 (coin), Teresa Kasprzycka, 13, Yu
Lan, 22 (flag), Yuri Yavnik, 1, 21, zhu difeng, 5, 7

Note to Parents and Teachers

The Countries set supports national social studies standards related to
people, places, and culture. This book describes and illustrates China. The
images support early readers in understanding the text. The repetition
of words and phrases helps early readers learn new words. This book
also introduces early readers to subject-specific vocabulary words, which
are defined in the Glossary section. Early readers may need assistance to
read some words and to use the Table of Contents, Glossary, Read More,
Internet Sites, and Index sections of the book.

Printed in the United States of America in North Mankato, Minnesota.
032013   007223CGF13

Table of Contents

Where Is China?

China is the fourth-biggest country in the world. It's a little smaller than the United States.

China is in eastern Asia. China's capital is Beijing.

Beijing ★

CHINA

Landforms and Climate

China has rivers, mountains, and deserts. Heavy rain helps plants grow along the Yangtze River. Snow falls in the Himalaya mountains. Winds blow across the Gobi Desert.

Animals

Many rare animals live only
in China. Giant pandas, golden
hair monkeys, South China tigers,
and Chinese alligators are
all at risk of dying out.

Language and Population

China is home to more than 1.3 billion people. Most people in China speak and write Mandarin Chinese. This language has thousands of symbols.

Food

The Chinese enjoy fresh vegetables, fish, and tea. They also eat soup, rice, and noodles. People in China eat with chopsticks.

Celebrations

Chinese New Year is celebrated in January or February. The holiday lasts for 15 days. People watch parades and fireworks. Some people dress in dragon costumes.

Where People Work

About half of China's people work as farmers. They grow rice, wheat, and tea. Some people have jobs catching fish. In cities most people work in factories.

Transportation

People ride bicycles in most cities
in China. Subways and buses
are busy too. People living
in mountains might use horses
to travel.

Famous Sight

The Great Wall of China is thousands of miles long. It's the biggest thing ever built by people. People from around the world visit the Great Wall every year.

Country Facts

Name: People's Republic of China

Capital: Beijing

Population: 1,349,585,838 (July 2013 estimate)

Size: 3,705,407 square miles
(9,596,960 square kilometers)

Language: Mandarin Chinese

Main Crops: rice, wheat, potatoes, corn, peanuts

Money: Yuan

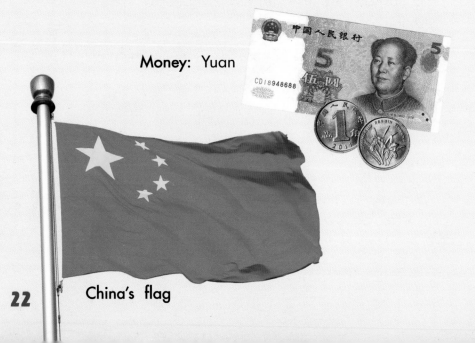

China's flag

Glossary

Asia—the largest of Earth's seven continents; a continent is a large landmass

capital—the city in a country where the government is based

Chinese New Year—the first day of the Chinese Lunar Calendar; the lunar calendar is based on the phases of the moon

chopsticks—narrow sticks used to eat food; chopsticks are used mostly by people in Asian countries

factory—the place where a product, such as a car, is made

language—the way people speak or talk

subway—a system of trains that runs underground in a city

symbol—a design or an object that stands for something else

Hardyman, Robyn. *China.* New York: Chelsea Clubhouse, 2009.

Noi, Goh Sui and Lim Bee Ling. *China.* New York: Marshall Cavendish Benchmark, 2011.

Simmons, Walter. *China.* Minneapolis: Bellwether Media, 2011.

Internet Sites

FactHound offers a safe, fun way to find Internet sites related to this book. All of the sites on FactHound have been researched by our staff.

Here's all you do:
Visit *www.facthound.com*
Type in this code: 9781476530772

Super-cool stuff!

Check out projects, games and lots more at
www.capstonekids.com

Index

Word Count: 227　　　Grade: 1　　　Early-Intervention Level: 18